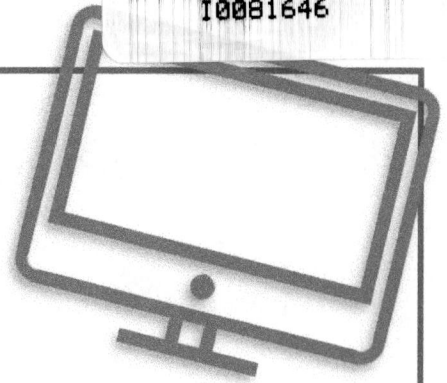

This book comes With Lots of **FREE and Additional Resources for Purchase**

Resources can be found on a page dedicated to this book on our website. Here you can:

DOWNLOAD WORKSHEETS: There are a few additional worksheets that can be downloaded for free.

GET UPDATES: If there are profound changes to the strategies printed in this book you will be the first to know when you join our monthly newsletter on our website.

JOIN OUR PRIVATE FACEBOOK GROUP: Interact with me on a regular basis and bounce ideas off likeminded individuals who have also purchased this book and are following the strategies.

TAKE THE COURSE: Yes, there is a comprehensive course that goes along with this book. We want to appeal to all types of learners and extend continued support and clarify the concepts like only face to face interactions can.

PURCHASE THE WORKBOOK: There is a step-by-step workbook that accompanies this book. The workbook is broken down into chapters just like this book is, with exercises for you to complete so that there is a correlation with what you have read and the steps you need to take to re-enforce the concepts.

WATCH THE VIDEOS: This is another free resource. The video library in the Facebook group has and abundance of information with real-life scenarios and effective strategies.

There's MORE!

We also have a directory of networking events and groups in your area with basic descriptions and contact information so that you can choose the one that's best for your business needs.

www.21irrefutablelawsofnetworking.com

What People Are Saying

This book is phenomenal. As an introvert and someone that doesn't really like networking, this book has equipped me with the necessary strategies to confidently and successfully network to increase my revenue and make new connections.
Tracy V. Allen, Impact Strategist – TVA Consulting, LLC

If you are nervous about networking as most people are, pick up 21 Irrefutable Laws of Networking. You will find some great tips that Denean shares with you to help you navigate and be more effective while networking.
Ronald L. Harvey, Vice President - GCS Consulting, LLC

This book is a real-life account of how networking works. As I read this book, I thought of the times I showed up unprepared; I did not take opportunities that were right there, my demeanor and even my tone. The part about saying (I'm sorry did I offend you) I like that. I've never said it, but it makes sense. I have shown up and said, "I'll wing it." Never ever will I do this again after reading your book. Outstanding job breaking it down!
Antoinette Davis

When you think about the essentials for running a successful business, networking should be at the top of the list. Denean has captured the key components to help every business owner, whether new or seasoned, grow their client-base, which will ultimately lead to growing a successful business. Before you plan another networking event or plan to attend one, this book should be read, to give you the skills to stand out and grow personally and professionally.
Tamika Washington, Community Manager & Founder of ConverSpace

21 Irrefutable Laws of Networking Workbook

Denean R. Ambersley

| Editor/Typesetter | Tracy V. Allen |
| Cover Design | Denean R. Ambersley |

For information on bulk purchases, please contact the Sales Department. Call (803)602-5358, Email info@deneanthecoffeequeen.com, or write to Denean R. Ambersley, 4611 Hard Scrabble Suite 109-266, Columbia, South Carolina 29229.

ISBN 978-0-578-67315-8

> ### *Please note*
>
> We have made every effort to provide you with accurate information that should help you grow your network and your business. None of the information in this book should be taken as legal advice. If you are looking for legal advice, please contact a licensed professional.

Acknowledgments

This four-year project does not just happen by accident, but by being intentional. I wrote this book with YOU in mind. So, I would like to thank everyone that purchases, reads, gifts, book us for a speaking engagement, and make recommendations to this project in advance.

First and foremost, I would like to thank God for creating my extraverted personality. Your presence in my life is a gift for me to share you with ALL. Your willingness to Love me for not only all of who I am but for all of who I can be in you, which motivates me to take bold actions in your space. I am committed to living the rest of my days for you and in you, leaving the witness of your Love in the world.

To my adult children, Donovan and Jenean Ambersley, for allowing me to raise you in a loving home, have a thriving career, and start a new business. At the same time, you stayed focused on your studies and careers while supporting mom as well. I truly appreciate you both for serving in the military, US Air Force, and US Navy respectfully for one term with honorable service. This makes both parents very proud.

To my best friends and sisters, Laura P. Diaz (RIH), Rachel Evans, and Darlene C. Hagood. If I begin to write about these ladies, tears, and a new book will emerge, so let me just acknowledge you for believing in and supporting me on this project.

As a John Maxwell Certified Speaker, Trainer, and Coach, I want to thank the John Maxwell Team for teaching me that Leadership means to influence, nothing more, nothing less, as I believe this book will influence your growth in Business and your Career.

I want to thank the Best Educator I know personally, Tracy V. Allen of TVA Consulting, for helping me with my writing style and book coaching. The pre-readers, my editors, and publisher for supporting my vision and helping me to share this gift with the world. It truly was a team effort.

I want to thank ALL of my military family, which means all branches of services as I served and fought beside them in Saudi Arabia, Afghanistan, and Kuwait regions. Even in wartime, we had to move the battles along through personnel management, communication, and networking.

To my Marketing Analyst, Princess Cooper, you've done so much for this Brand that it is now on the map and definitely going in the right direction as your vision always overwhelms me with joy. You have my permission to create it in your own way…remember, just create me something Emerald, then have your way.

To the best Executive Administrator, Pam Felder, of Connecting Concepts, thanks for taking so much off my plate inside of Denean The Coffee Queen, LLC, A Healthy Beverage Company, so that I could donate time to this major project. Now, the work begins!

To Taurea Vision Avant of Show Your Success, LLC, who first believed in and gave me an opportunity to become a Best-Selling Author as a collaborator of Multiple Streams of Income by Denean R. Ambersley. What you do for new Authors will leave legacies and great how-to content in the Marketplace.

To my Clients and Customers. You Rock! This is how I describe my clients and customers, because of the Customer Service we provide to them, they always show up in support, and for their delicious, healthier coffee, cocoa, and teas. Now, it's time for Referrals, so please take a moment and think about great referrals just like yourself.

I am forever grateful for knowing this is not my home, but when I get called up, I truly pray this would be a legacy, along with my Faith left for my children's children for generations to come.

Denean R. Ambersley,

- Affectionately known as Denean The Coffee Queen

About the Author

Denean R. Ambersley is the author of the Best-Selling book "Multiple Streams of Income" has done it again through practical research, practiced networking, and documenting, "21 Irrefutable Laws of Networking – Let's Meet for Coffee," actions that work. Denean has traveled around the world as a U.S. Army Veteran, touching four continents and flying over all 7 Seas; in doing so, she has connected with, trained, and has given many keynote speeches to millions of Soldiers, Family members, and Civilians. Her travels have allowed for extensive Networking opportunities that have helped her to understand the value of meeting people and leaving them with a positive impression that leads to a lasting connection. Some of her favorite sayings are, "Teamwork makes the dream work" and "no man is an island" are not just clichés but reality.

Denean is the Chief Executive Officer of Denean The Coffee Queen LLC, a healthier beverage company. She believes that after meeting someone for the first time, the next step is to meet them for a cup of coffee; even if you drink coffee, tea, or water, the invite is, "Let's meet for coffee." At this meeting, the magic begins, and this book and workbook will help you hone in on your skills to become a master networker, team builder, and connector all in one. After reading this book, working through the workbook, and putting all that you have learned into practice, very soon, you will notice that you are 6-degrees separated from that person you have always wanted to work with or meet. People such as your local Mayor, the Pope, a Movie Star, the CEO of a Fortune 500 Company, and possibly the President of the United States. Enjoy your journey, but please keep a Rolodex (contact list) for every person that you have left an impression on, and that has left an impression on you.

Table of Contents

Law 1

The Law of The Main Thing

Networking is the ability to connect and interact with other people to exchange information and develop contacts to advance one's business/career. Your ability to network effectively can be the determining factor between the advancement or failure of your new or established business or career endeavors. Identifying "The Main Thing" will help to keep you focus as you venture into networking for the purpose of building your contact lists and partnerships.

You cannot allow your inability to network effectively to be the deciding factor in your lack of success.

REFLECT

Let's explore some questions that will help you figure out your effectiveness or lack thereof when it comes to networking.

1. Do you like networking?   Why or Why not?

   _____

   _____

   _____

   _____

2. How many networking events do you attend per quarter? (List)

   _____   _____

   _____   _____

   _____   _____

3. How many meaningful contacts are you creating from these events? Explain why they are meaningful.

    _____

    _____

    _____

    _____

4. What type of networking events are you attending? Paid or Free? How much are the paid events? Which one(s) do you find most effective?

    _____

    _____

    _____

    _____

    _____

    _____

5. What kind of networking events are you attending? Industry or General? Why are you attending each one and which have been most success for making new contacts for you?

    _____

    _____

    _____

    _____

6. What was your first networking experience?

    _____

    _____

    _____

    _____

7. What is your most vivid memory of that experience?

    _____

    _____

    _____

    _____

8. What do you think you did correctly at that meeting?

_____

_____

_____

_____

9. What do you think you did incorrectly?

_____

_____

_____

_____

10. Is there a way that you could have improved upon the experience? If so, what could you have done?

_____

_____

_____

_____

_____

_____

_____

Why are you showing up?

1. What is your why for networking? Explain and list your top 3 reasons.

_____

_____

_____

A. _____

B. _____

C. _____

2. Who's showing up with you at these networking events that you are attending? Name them by profession.

1. _____   3. _____

2. _____   4. _____

5. _____   6. _____

3. Who do you need to show up for the experience to be worthwhile? Name them by profession.

1. _____   4. _____

2. _____   5. _____

3. _____   6. _____

Be Intentional

1. Based on the reading, you know that you must approach every meeting with precise intention in order to achieve the desired outcome. What are your intentions for networking?

1. _____   2. _____

3. _____   4. _____

5. _____   6. _____

Outcomes

1. What outcomes if any have you received from prior networking events?

   1. _____ 2. _____
      _____   _____
   3. _____ 4. _____
      _____   _____

2. With the knowledge that you have acquired in this chapter, what are your desired outcomes for your next networking event?

   1. _____ 2. _____
      _____   _____
   3. _____ 4. _____
      _____   _____

STRATEGIZE

Based on the information you learned in this chapter, what do you plan to do differently when you attend your next networking event?

Event: _____ Time: _____

Day: _____ Location: _____

1. Who's going to be at the event that you want to meet? (Person or People)

_____

_____

2. How are you going to find out information on these people?

_____

_____

_____

_____

3. How is this connection going to be mutually beneficial?

_____

_____

_____

4. How do you plan on acquiring their contact information and stay in-touch?

_____

_____

_____

_____

EVALUATE

What was the outcome of the networking event that you strategized about after completing this workbook lesson, Law 1: "The Law of The Main Thing?"

- Write a detailed synopsis of how this event was different from others that you have been to in the past?
- Describe what type and kind of networking event you attended.
- Note how many contacts you were able to make (not business cards collected).
- Who did you follow up with, and what were the results?
- Was the reconnaissance you did on the people you wanted to meet at the event helpful to networking more effectively?
- Add any other details that you think are significant to the networking experience.

Law 2
The Law of Networking

You must set clear goals and plot a path to obtaining it. Find out what works for you and where you feel most comfortable and work it to achieve your goals.

In this section, you will be plotting out your next major networking event to make sure that you are prepared with all of the arsenals needed to mesmerize your targets and walk away with follow up meetings over coffee.

REFLECT

Let's explore some questions that will help you figure out your purpose for networking. How has it helped you? What is your why?

1. Why have you been attending networking events? Dig deep and figure out if you had a conscious and explicit purpose for attending those events? Write your answer in detail.

_____

_____

_____

_____

_____

_____

_____

_____

_____

Who, What, When, Where, How, Calendar

1. Who have you networked with to get what you wanted and desired?

_____

_____

_____

2. Do you have any idea who you needed to be in contact with to achieve your desired outcome before you attended the event?

_____

_____

_____

3. What do you think you needed to know about the people you desire to network with before you actually meet them that you didn't know?

_____

_____

_____

_____

_____

4. When have you found to be the best time to network with the people that you desire and why?

_____

_____

_____

5. Where have you been going to meet the people you need to connect with for growth and expansion?

Formal Networking Events:

_____

_____

_____

Unstructured: (E.g. Restaurant, Bar, Church, etc.)

_____

_____

_____

6. How did you prepare for your first encounter with this person especially in an environment that was not a networking event?

_____

_____

_____

7. Did you create a calendar to track your networking events and progress? Fill in this information based on your past experiences.

BEFORE THE EVENT:

Date of the Event _____

Event Time _____

Length _____

Who is having the event? _____

Where is the event? _____

Cost of the event? _____

Who do you want to meet? Concentrate on building a rapport with only 3 people.

1. _____(Name)

   _____(Industry)

   _____ (Why do you want to meet them)

   _____ (What will be your approach)

2. _____(Name)

   _____(Industry)

   _____ (Why do you want to meet them)

   _____ (What will be your approach)

3. _____(Name)

   _____(Industry)

   _____ (Why do you want to meet them)

   _____ (What will be your approach)

What is your primary purpose in going to the event?

_____

_____

_____

AFTER THE EVENT:

Number of people that attended the event. _____

Who did you actually connect with?

1. _____(Name)

   _____(Industry)

   _____ (Who approached who)

   _____ (Key points to remember)

2. _____(Name)

   _____(Industry)

   _____ (Who approached who)

   _____ (Key points to remember)

3. _____(Name)

   _____(Industry)

   _____ (Who approached who)

   _____ (Key points to remember)

What did you like about the event?

_____

_____

_____

What didn't you like about the event?

_____

_____

_____

Would you attend the event again? Why or why not?

_____

_____

_____

Who is on your coffee list?

1. _____(Name)

   _____(Industry)

   _____ (Who approached who)

   _____ (Key points to remember)

   _____ (Follow up: Date/Avenue)

   _____ (Meet up: When & Where)

   _____ (Result of the Meet up)

_____ (Next Steps)

2. _____(Name)

_____(Industry)

_____ (Who approached who)

_____ (Key points to remember)

_____ (Follow up: Date/Avenue)

_____ (Meet up: When & Where)

_____ (Result of the Meet up)

_____ (Next Steps)

3. _____(Name)

_____(Industry)

_____ (Who approached who)

_____ (Key points to remember)

_____ (Follow up: Date/Avenue)

_____ (Meet up: When & Where)

_____ (Result of the Meet up)

_____ (Next Steps)

Events – Chamber, Major Industry

What chamber of commerce, BNI, or other industry specific events have you attended in the last 3-months? What did you like and dislike about each? Would you want to attend another event there? Why or Why not?

1. _____

_____

_____

2. _____
   _____
   _____

3. _____
   _____
   _____

Like, Know, and Trust

How did you approach the getting to know, like, and trust factor? What was your approach when meeting your target for the first time?

_____
_____
_____
_____
_____

Charitable Organizations
Rotary Club

Have you attended any charitable or rotary club organization events? If so, what was the positives and negatives of the event and the experience?

_____
_____
_____

Connecting Over Coffee

Of all the events that you attended in the last 3-months, how many of them resulted in a coffee meet-up? List the people you connected with, where you met them, why they resonated with you, what lead to the coffee meet-up, and what was the result of the meet-up.

Person #1

Name _____ Business _____

Initial Meeting Place _____

What made this person attractive enough to talk to? _____

_____

_____

What lead to the coffee meet-up? – Who reached out first and how long after the event?

_____

What was the objective of the coffee meet-up?

Yours. _____

_____

Theirs. _____

_____

How long was the meeting? Was a hard stop discussed? _____

Did the meet-up go as planned? Explain. _____

_____

_____

Key conversational points. _____

_____

_____

_____

Would you meet-up with this person again? Why or why not? _____

_____

_____

Have you gotten any business or referrals from this person? Explain if necessary.

_____

_____

Did you give any referrals to this person? Explain if necessary. _____

_____

_____

Person #2

Name _____ Business _____

Initial Meeting Place _____

What made this person attractive enough to talk to? _____

_____

_____

What lead to the coffee meet-up? – Who reached out first and how long after the event?

_____

What was the objective of the coffee meet-up?

Yours. _____

_____

Theirs. _____

_____

How long was the meeting? Was a hard stop discussed? _____

Did the meet-up go as planned? Explain. _____

_____

_____

Key conversational points. _____

_____

_____

_____

Would you meet-up with this person again? Why or why not? _____

_____

_____

Have you gotten any business or referrals from this person? Explain if necessary.

_____

_____

Did you give any referrals to this person? Explain if necessary. _____

_____

_____

Person #3

Name _____ Business _____

Initial Meeting Place _____

What made this person attractive enough to talk to? _____

_____

What lead to the coffee meet-up? – Who reached out first and how long after the event?

_____

What was the objective of the coffee meet-up?

Yours. _____

_____

Theirs. _____

_____

How long was the meeting? Was a hard stop discussed? _____

Did the meet-up go as planned? Explain. _____

_____

_____

Key conversational points. _____

_____

_____

_____

Would you meet-up with this person again? Why or why not? _____

_____

_____

Have you gotten any business or referrals from this person? Explain if necessary.

_____

_____

Did you give any referrals to this person? Explain if necessary. _____

_____

_____

Person #4

Name _____ Business _____

Initial Meeting Place _____

What made this person attractive enough to talk to? _____

_____

_____

What lead to the coffee meet-up? – Who reached out first and how long after the event?

_____

What was the objective of the coffee meet-up?

Yours. _____

_____

Theirs. _____

_____

How long was the meeting? Was a hard stop discussed? _____

Did the meet-up go as planned? Explain. _____

_____

_____

Key conversational points. _____

_____

_____

_____

Would you meet-up with this person again? Why or why not? _____

_____

_____

Have you gotten any business or referrals from this person? Explain if necessary.

_____

_____

Did you give any referrals to this person? Explain if necessary. _____

_____

_____

STRATEGIZE

So, the point of this exercise is to help you hone in on the reason that you are networking. Be very velar about your goals and expectations below. Remember, do NOT plan on connecting with more than 3-4 people at a networking event that you genuinely want to follow up with later. You don't want networking and following up to take away from your other revenue-generating activities.

After doing your initial reconnaissance, who are you planning on connecting with, why, and how (practice how you will introduce yourself and what you will tell them about themselves to let them know that you have done your homework in a non-creepy way)? Create your action plan using the format below.

Who is on your coffee list?

1. _____(Name)

   _____ (Business Name)

   _____ (Years in Business)

   _____(Location)

   _____(Industry)

   _____ (Signature Product)

   _____ (Clients they've worked with)

   _____ (Clients they've worked with)

   _____ (Clients they've worked with)

_____

_____

_____

(What will you say when you approach them – Your 30-second pitch – Not Sales)

_____

_____

_____

(What will you say when you approach them – Your 30-second pitch [about their company])

_____

_____

_____

2. _____(Name)

_____ (Business Name)

_____ (Years in Business)

_____(Location)

_____(Industry)

_____ (Signature Product)

_____ (Clients they've worked with)

_____ (Clients they've worked with)

_____ (Clients they've worked with)

_____

_____

_____

(What will you say when you approach them – Your 30-second pitch – Not Sales)

_____

_____

_____

(What will you say when you approach them – Your 30-second pitch [about their company])

_____

_____

_____

3. _____(Name)

_____ (Business Name)

_____ (Years in Business)

_____(Location)

_____(Industry)

_____ (Signature Product)

_____ (Clients they've worked with)

_____ (Clients they've worked with)

_____ (Clients they've worked with)

_____

_____

_____

(What will you say when you approach them – Your 30-second pitch - Not Sales)

_____

_____

_____

(What will you say when you approach them – Your 30-second pitch [about their company])

_____

_____

_____

EVALUATE

After all your preparations, reflect on what happened at the event.
Did preparing help? _____

_____

_____

_____

_____

Where they receptive to your spiels? Explain. _____

_____

_____

_____

_____

Will you be reaching out to them again? Why or why not? (Sometimes after having a live, 1:1, conversation with someone you might realize they are not what they may have appeared to be publicly).

_____

_____

_____

_____

_____

What could you have done differently? _____

_____

_____

_____

_____

What will you try the next time? _____

_____

_____

_____

_____

Law 3

The Law of Attraction

How are you showing up? Your appearance matters. How you present yourself physically matters to the people that you meet. No matter how shallow you may think it is, it matters. If you are honest, it matters to you as well how people are showing up in your space. The way you look when someone sees you for the first time is usually the way they see you all the time. That image is permanently implanted in their minds.

In this section, we will evaluate how you and others are showing up in networking spaces and what it says about you before you even say hello.

REFLECT

1. What do you usually do to prepare physically before a networking event?

_____

_____

_____

Hair _____   Clothing _____

Nails _____   Shoes _____

Make Up _____   Accessories _____

Oral Hygiene _____   Physical Hygiene _____

Other _____   Other _____

Who do you want to attract?

When assessing others physically at an event, what does their physical appearance say to you about them before you engage in a conversation?

_____

_____

_____

How does this affect your view of yourself? _____

_____

_____

How does it affect your interaction with that person when you have the opportunity to speak? _____

_____

_____

Clothing

Are you a brand watcher? Are you in a room with brand watchers? Does it really matter what brand someone is wearing or carrying? Does this influence your interaction with people at the event? Do you think it affects the way they interact with you?

_____

_____

_____

_____

_____

_____

Is clean, pressed, and well-coordinated more impressive than name brands to you? Why?

_____

_____

_____

Hygiene

What does the hygiene of the person you are meeting say to you about that person's professionalism? Does it have any influence on your perception of them?

_____

_____

_____

When you meet people with poor hygiene at networking events does it make you work harder to make sure that your bodily orders are not off putting?

_____

_____

_____

STRATEGIZE

Create a game plan for showing up to networking event looking and smelling like you are ready to do business especially if you are coming directly from work or have been running errands all day.

_____

_____

_____

Hair _____   Clothing _____

Nails _____   Shoes _____

Make Up _____   Accessories _____

Oral Hygiene _____   Physical Hygiene _____

Other _____   Other _____

EVALUATE

Journal your assessment of physical appearance and personal hygiene on your perception and decisions to work with or not with someone you meet at a networking event. Be brutally honest in your assessment of your reaction and come up with solutions to combat it in the event that these circumstances present again. Remember we want to treat people the way we want to be treated.

_____

_____

_____

_____

_____

_____

_____

_____

_____

_____

_____

_____

_____

_____

_____

_____

_____

_____

_____

_____

_____

_____

Law 4

The Law of Introvert & Extravert

The comfort zone is the most comforting and secure space to be in, but it can also be the most damaging space to be in as well. Most people find immense bliss in their comfort zone. Why? It is safe and predictable.

So, why do you need to step as far outside of your comfort zone as possible? You need to grow and create revenue. The only way to do that is to get uncomfortable.

In this section, we will explore stepping out and becoming uncomfortable.

REFLECT

1. What is your normal course of action when it comes to interacting with people you don't know? E.g. Avoid them, Stutter, Freeze, etc.

   _____

   _____

   _____

   _____

2. How has this course of action worked for you in the pass? What type of feedback have you received?

   _____

   _____

   _____

3. Describe a situation when you took a risk and stepped outside you comfort zone.

   _____

   _____

   _____

   _____

_____

_____

4. Explain the outcome and what you learned from it.

_____

_____

_____

_____

_____

_____

Personality Traits

What do you feel are your personality traits?

1. _____ 4. _____

2. _____ 5. _____

3. _____ 6. _____

What personality traits have people told you that you possess?

1. _____ 4. _____

2. _____ 5. _____

3. _____ 6. _____

Do you feel that your traits and theirs are similar or different?

_____

_____

_____

If different, have you ever taken the time to assess the energy that you are projecting when you are around others? Have you tried to curve any of the negative ones without changing who you are at the core? _____

_____

_____

_____

What were the results of your personality experiment? _____

_____

_____

What personality traits do you think that you are attracted to the most? Why?

_____

_____

_____

_____

What personality traits are attracted to you?

_____

_____

_____

_____

Stay In vs. Going Out

Are you a home-body – some who would prefer to stay indoors and not interact with the masses (introvert)?

_____

_____

_____

How has this behavior affected your business? _____

_____

_____

Are you extremely social on social media – making new and meaningful connection there often? _____

_____

_____

Do you like socializing with others? How often do you interact in structured and unstructured social setting each month? _____

In your structured networking groups are you making connections? _____

Are you keeping in contact with these connections? _____

Work on Your Weakness

What are your identified weaknesses?

_____

_____

_____

What weakness have you been told you have? _____

_____

_____

What have you done to strengthen your weaknesses in the past? _____

_____

_____

_____

STRATEGIZE

After you have identified your weaknesses, create a plan of action to turn those weakness into a strength or less of a threat. Use the space below to create that plan.

_____

_____

_____

_____

_____

_____

_____

_____

_____

_____

_____

_____

EVALUATE

After you've taken some time to implement your plan of action above, what changes in your interactions did you notice. Has it made a difference in the amount of authentic connections you have been able to create leading to more referrals and revenue?

_____

_____

_____

_____

_____

_____

_____

_____

_____

Law 5

The Law of the Meeting

If you are still attending networking events by happenstance, that is a habit that you need to break immediately. Is it working for you? Are you garnering any results from going to networking events whenever the mood hits you, or have you been strategic?

Attending networking events is like preparing for a tactical mission. Yes, it is that serious if you intend to use networking to elevate you to the next level and expand your network with meaningful connections.

In this section, we will explore how you can start planning for success.

REFLECT

1. In previous chapters we discussed knowing who you want to network with when you go to networking events. After going through those exercises, you are knowledgeable about who you need to network with for success. Please explain your target and ideal person.

   _____

   _____

   _____

   _____

   _____

   _____

   _____

   _____

2. What are you doing to prepare for the events that you are going to?

_____

_____

3. How are you finding and choosing these events?

_____

_____

_____

The Agenda - Place in Book

Do you have an agenda book? _____

If yes, how are you setting it up for success? _____

_____

_____

If no, here is a template you can use. – **See Next Page**

Date _____

Time _____ - _____

Event _____

Address _____

Type _____

Organizer _____

Contact Info _____

Target #1 _____

  Industry _____

  Why _____

Target #2 _____

  Industry _____

  Why _____

Target #3 _____

  Industry _____

  Why _____

Date _____

Time _____ - _____

Event _____

Address _____

Type _____

Organizer _____

Contact Info _____

Target #1 _____

  Industry _____

  Why _____

Target #2 _____

  Industry _____

  Why _____

Target #3 _____

  Industry _____

  Why _____

Date _____

Time _____ - _____

Event _____

Address _____

Type _____

Organizer _____

Contact Info _____

Target #1 _____

  Industry _____

  Why _____

Target #2 _____

  Industry _____

  Why _____

Target #3 _____

  Industry _____

  Why _____

Date _____

Time _____ - _____

Event _____

Address _____

Type _____

Organizer _____

Contact Info _____

Target #1 _____

  Industry _____

  Why _____

Target #2 _____

  Industry _____

  Why _____

Target #3 _____

  Industry _____

  Why _____

Location - Coffee Shop, Neutral Ground

Do you have a favorite coffee shop? Is it easily accessible and somewhat quiet? Are there tables where you can have a meeting for about an hour in comfort?

_____

_____

_____

How have your prior meetings at this location gone? (Remember, whenever possible, use a locally owned coffee shop. You are a small business, so you should support other small businesses). _____

_____

_____

Who Pays?

Do you pay when you invite someone to coffee, or do you let them pay for themselves? Why?

_____

_____

_____

If you are paying do you let them get a pastry as well? _____

What is you cap for paying? _____

Coffee vs. Golf Course

Have you met at the golf course instead of for coffee? If yes, why there? _____
_____
_____

If you have, (you both play golf) has this experience been more successful for you than a coffee meet-up? _____
_____
_____

Have you reflected on the literal cost and benefits of meeting at either place? _____
- How much are you spending at the golf course? _____
- How much business are you getting from golf course meetings? _____
- How much are spending at the coffee shop? _____
- How much business are you getting from coffee shop meetings? _____

Which was more beneficial financially from this analysis? _____

Other reflection on this matter from a personal prospective. _____
_____
_____

STRATEGIZE

After reflecting above, create a plan that details how you will determine who you meet where. Is golf on your radar or is the local coffee shop more your style? Make sure to include the factors (personal, financial, etc.) that will influence your decision.

_____
_____

_____

_____

_____

_____

_____

_____

_____

_____

_____

_____

EVALUATE

After you've taken some time to implement your plan of action above, journal the changes you have experienced in the amount of business or referrals that you have received based on the strategy? Is your ROI any greater?

_____

_____

_____

_____

_____

_____

_____

_____

_____

_____

_____

_____

_____

Law 6
The Law of Relationships

Building meaningful relationships is the only way to succeed in life. As much as we would like to think that we can build our businesses and career as loners, we find that it becomes a desolate and tall hill to climb when no hands are being extended out to help us up.

In this section, we will explore ways in which you can build authentic, meaningful relationships that are like a gift that keeps on giving.

REFLECT

1. Is it hard for you to create meaningful connects that generate lasting business relations that may eventually turn into friendships?

   _____

   _____

   _____

   _____

2. How much social interaction are you partaking in on a weekly basis? What type?

   _____

   _____

   _____

3. Are any of these interactions creating revenue or referrals for you? Explain.

   _____

   _____

   _____

   _____

_____

_____

The Morning After

What do you do the morning after a networking event? List what you do in order with the contacts (Business Cards/LinkedIn Connections) you have gathered.

1. _____   4. _____

2. _____   5. _____

3. _____   6. _____

How does the above activities help you to solidify the relationships you want to germinate? _____

_____

_____

Are We Related?

Of the people that you have connected with in the past, what makes you feel a kinship to them? _____

_____

_____

What levels did you relate and connect with to build upon? _____

_____

_____

Would you like a second date?

How many second date have you been on? _____

What made these second dates worth scheduling, meaningful, and successful?

_____

_____

The second dates that never happened - why? _____

_____

_____

STRATEGIZE

Here is the bare minimum of what you should be doing the morning after each networking event.

The Morning After Checklist:

☐ Create a list of the people you met and decide which are going to be of value to you based on your initial conversation. Remember, not everyone needs to be in your circle. Exhibit discernment.

☐ Make sure you email all the people you met and exchanged cards with and felt a connection strong enough to warrant a follow-up.

☐ Set up coffee dates with the ones you want to get to know better by creating a phone call.

Keep a log of your interaction like the one in chapter 2. Journal about your experiences below.

_____

_____

_____

_____

_____

_____

_____

_____

_____

_____

_____

EVALUATE

What have you learned about the way you build relationship and who you are attracted to the most based on past and present experiences? Explain in detail.

_____

_____

_____

_____

_____

_____

_____

_____

_____

_____

_____

Law 7

The Law of Networking
on Social Media

Social media is a powerful tool that has made this vast world so much smaller. It allows people to connect with you and learn who you are in a new and noninvasive way. It can help you realize existing connections you have with potential networkers and learn all about them before meeting them at the event.

With that in mind, in this section, we will explore a few tips to help you network more effectively with social media.

REFLECT

1. Are you active on social media? _____

   What social media platforms do you have a business page on?

   _____ _____ _____

   _____ _____ _____

2. How many days per week are you actively posting about your business? _____

3. What is your engagement like on these platforms? _____

   _____

   _____

4. How many followers do you have on each of these platforms? _____

   _____ _____ _____

5. How many of these people have you engaged (networked) with in the Direct Messenger (DM)? _____

_____

_____

6. What were the results of these interactions? _____

_____

_____

_____

Personal Pages/Business Pages/Groups

Do you have any Facebook or LinkedIn Groups of your own? _____

How successful is this group? Does it have a lot of engagement? Are you getting new business from it? _____

_____

_____

How many industry-specific groups are you involved in on any platform? _____

Are you actively engaged in any of these groups? (posting, commenting, sharing) How often?

_____

_____

If you are not active in any of these groups why not? _____

_____

_____

Blogs/Vlogs/Podcast

Do you have a blog/vlog/podcast? Which one or ones?

_____

_____

_____

How often are you posting on these platforms? _____

_____   _____

Are you using any of the above to connect with other industry experts and clientele?

_____

How are you maintaining the relationship with those that interact with your blog, vlog, or podcast?

_____

_____

_____

Maintain Professional Relationships

How have you been maintaining the relationships that could possibly develop from the engagement on your various platforms?

_____

_____

_____

Identify Leaders and Organizations

How are you using these platforms to identify leaders/decision makers in the industry?

_____

_____

_____

How are you reaching out to them? _____

_____

_____

When you get a response are you following up with in person or through virtual coffee shop meet-ups? _____

_____

_____

_____

Are you asking them out on second and third dates to solidify the relationship?

_____

How many of these relationships have you been able to maintain? How? Explain.

_____

_____

STRATEGIZE

Create a plan to use your groups to build relationships. Find at least 2-3 people that look like they would be interesting to get to know. Do the same reconnaissance that you would for a live networking event and then reach out to them in the DM's. Follow the same format discussed in previous chapters. Use the charts in the other chapter to log the information you gathered in the space below to create that plan.

_____

_____

_____

_____

_____

_____

_____

_____

_____

_____

_____

_____

Create a plan to connect with the people who leave messages on you blog, vlog, podcast, or social media post. You don't want to get into the DM's of everyone, but you do want to use some discernment to determine which ones are worth reaching out to privately. Use the space below to create the criteria for who you will reach out to and who you won't. _____

_____

_____

_____

_____

_____

_____

_____

_____

_____

_____

_____

_____

_____

_____

_____

_____

_____

EVALUATE

After you've implemented your new strategies, journal what has worked and what hasn't. Create a plan for tweaking what hasn't worked to be more effective.

_____

_____

_____

_____

_____

_____

_____

_____

_____

_____

_____

_____

_____

_____

_____

_____

_____

_____

_____

_____

_____

_____

_____

_____

Law 8

The Law of the Follow Up

Timing is essential when following-up after a networking event. Following up helps you to solidify your relationships. You should follow-up within 24-48 hours via email. Following up also gives you a chance to express appreciation for their time, restate the important details from your conversation, ask clarifying questions, or arrange a time to meet over coffee.

In this section, we will explore ways to follow-up that yields an ROI.

REFLECT

1. Do you follow-up with people you meet at networking events? How often?

   _____

   _____

2. How quickly do you make the initial follow-up on average? And what mode do you use to connect? (Email, Social Media, etc.) _____

   _____

   _____

3. Are you using key talking points from your initial conversation to help the person remember who you are and where you met? _____

   _____

   _____

   _____

4. Are you proofreading before pressing send? _____

5. Are you asking for a follow up meeting as a coffee date in the initial follow up?

_____

_____

6. What is your success rate currently? Explain. _____

_____

_____

7. Is there anything else that you have noticed? _____

_____

_____

8. Do you have a standard letter that you use to follow up and tweak to the specific instance? The one provided in the book is great to use. _____

The Fortune is in the Follow-up

We all know nothing happens without the proper follow-up. Explain how you are following up after any form of networking on each of the platforms? What results are you getting from the follow-ups - referrals, new business, and B2B relationships?

Email _____

_____

_____

LinkedIn _____

_____

_____

Facebook _____

_____

_____

Twitter _____

_____

_____

Instagram _____

_____

_____

Other _____

_____

_____

STRATEGIZE

Use the letters provided in the book to help you create a standard format for following up via email or social media Direct Messenger (DMs).

- Determine when you will follow up via phone.

- Determine when is the right time to follow them on social media and get in their DMs.

- Determine how many times you will follow up before you stop trying.

_____

_____

_____

_____

_____

_____

_____

_____

_____

_____

_____

_____

_____

EVALUATE

After you've taken some time to implement your new strategy, journal how it has worked and what didn't work and how you will tweak it?

_____

_____

_____

_____

_____

_____

_____

_____

_____

_____

_____

_____

_____

_____

_____

_____

_____

_____

_____

_____

_____

_____

_____

_____

_____

Law 9

The Law of Influence

Influence is applying power to accomplish a specific purpose. Influence, in essence, is the power of manipulation. That manipulation can be dark or positive. Positive influence can help you to connect with the people you need to push you toward success in the world of networking.

In this section, we will explore how to connect with influential people and become influential yourself.

REFLECT

1. How are you determining who is influential enough for you to contact? What traits do they need to possess for you to consider them influential? Is it their social media following, business success, popularity?

   _____

   _____

   _____

   _____

2. How do you think that you can become influential in your own right? Have you ever created a strategy? Explain. _____

   _____

   _____

3. What steps have you tried?

   1. _____   4. _____

   2. _____   5. _____

   3. _____   6. _____

Logical approaches to Influencing

After reading the chapter which logical approach to influencing are you currently employing? Explain. _____
_____
_____
_____

Social approaches to Influencing

After reading the chapter which social approach to influencing are you currently employing? Explain. _____
_____
_____
_____

Emotional approaches to Influencing

After reading the chapter which emotional approach to influencing are you currently employing? Explain. _____
_____
_____
_____

STRATEGIZE

Now that you have assessed what your current approaches are, would it make sense to your success to curve your approach or adapt a new one that won't take you completely out of character? Explain.

_____

_____

_____

Create a strategy for each one, whether you are thinking of changing or planning to stick to what you are currently doing. All plans can be tweaked.

Logical _____

_____

_____

_____

Social _____

_____

_____

_____

Emotional _____

_____

_____

_____

What steps are you going to take to become more influential? (Doing more social media Lives or recorded videos, doing more speaking engagements, being more social by attending more networking events.) Explain.

_____

_____

_____
_____
_____
_____
_____
_____
_____
_____
_____
_____
_____

What is going to be your strategy for reaching out to and engaging with influencers in person or on social media?

_____
_____
_____
_____
_____
_____
_____
_____

EVALUATE

After you've taken some time to implement your strategies, explain how the changes have affected your influence and how it has helped you to interact with other influential people? _____

_____
_____
_____
_____
_____

Law 10

The Law of Sex Transmutation

I know it may seem strange to talk about sex in a book about networking, but just like we discussed earlier, networking is a lot like dating. When dating, we exhibit a lot of sexual energy. This sexual energy is also exhibited consciously or unconsciously when we are networking and meeting people for the first time. So, YES, we need to talk about sex or sexual energy when networking.

In this section, we will explore how sex transmutation affects you and your ability to network effectively.

REFLECT

After reading the chapter, what are your thoughts on sex transmutation and how it has been affecting your networking ROI either positively or negatively. Make sure to focus on your Power, Energy, and Creativity.

_____

_____

_____

_____

_____

_____

_____

_____

_____

_____

_____

_____

STRATEGIZE

Using the following steps to prepare a plan that will help you to exude confidence and manifest your desired outcome through sex transmutation.

Step 1: Be clear about your wants. Determine your goal(s):

1. What is your goal? _____
    _____
    _____

2. How do you visualize it happening? _____
    _____
    _____

3. How will you celebrate the outcome(s)? _____
    _____
    _____

Step 2: Focus squarely on the goal.

What outside forces will you have to contend with to make your goal a reality?

_____
_____
_____
_____

What will you give up to make this goal a reality? _____
_____
_____
_____
_____

How will you connect with your "why" and stay focused on your purpose for achieving it? _____

_____

_____

_____

Step 3: Be patient and remain focused.

How do you intend to stay focused through this process to achieve the desired outcome?

_____

_____

_____

_____

_____

_____

_____

_____

_____

_____

_____

_____

_____

EVALUATE

Evaluate and journal how each stage has worked for you. Remember that no plan is casted in stone and the point of an evaluation is to figure what worked in the implementation stage and what didn't and tweak them to make the process more effortless. _____

_____

_____

_____

Law 11

The Law of Showing Up Prepared

Although we have explored showing up prepared at networking events in previous chapters, I find the need to reinforce it here again. Showing up prepared at a networking event is imperative to the success of your business, your reputation, and the first impression you leave in the minds of those you meet.

In this section, we will be reinforcing the strategies you have learned about showing up prepared.

REFLECT

1. What networking faux pas have you engaged in? Where, when, and why did it happen? _____

_____

_____

_____

_____

_____

_____

_____

2. How did you recover to save face at the event or the next day? _____

_____

_____

_____

_____

_____

STRATEGIZE

Make sure to use the logs provided for you in other chapter to prevent you from showing up unprepared to a networking event. Take the time to write about the last networking event you attended and how showing up prepared made a difference. Compare and contrast the differences between unprepared and prepared. Map a strategy for continued success.

_____

_____

_____

_____

_____

_____

_____

_____

EVALUATE

After you've taken some time to implement your plan of action above highlight the changes you have recognized and how it has affected your connectivity, continued relationship building, referrals, and revenue.

_____

_____

_____

_____

_____

_____

_____

Law 12
The Law of Givers Gain

No matter what product or service you offer to the public, you have the opportunity to apply the "Givers Gain" method to your industry.

In this section, we will explore how you can give freely and gain a lot.

REFLECT

1. What have you done for free at a reduced price in order to gain new clients, make new connections, grow your email list? _____
   _____
   _____
   _____
   _____

2. How did it make you feel? _____
   _____

3. Would you do it or something like it again? Why or why not?
   _____
   _____
   _____
   _____

4. What boundary and negotiation lessons have you learned when doing something for free or at a reduced price?
   _____
   _____

_____

_____

_____

_____

STRATEGIZE

Based on what you wrote above and using the skill you have already learned from this chapter and previous chapters, what will be your strategy if you are approached again with an opportunity to Give? What do you want your Get to be? What will be your prepared spiel?

_____

_____

_____

_____

_____

_____

_____

_____

_____

_____

_____

_____

_____

_____

_____

_____

_____

EVALUATE

How well did your plan work when you were approached? Did you feel more equipped to handle the situation and negotiate an ROI that benefited your company?

_____

_____

_____

_____

_____

_____

_____

_____

_____

_____

_____

_____

_____

_____

_____

_____

_____

_____

_____

_____

_____

_____

_____

_____

_____

Law 13

The Law of Selling in the Marketplace

You sell by listening is my motto. You don't know what your customers want or how they want it if you aren't listening to what your customers are saying implicitly or explicitly. If you are not listening to what your current and potential customers are saying and doing, you are setting your business up for imminent failure.

In this section, we will explore why and how listening can elevate your networking and business success.

REFLECT

1. What have your customers or potential customers told you about want they wanted or needed from your business?

   _____

   _____

   _____

   _____

2. How did they tell you? _____

   Survey _____ Comment _____

   Testimonial _____

   Question _____

   Other _____

3. What has been the most requested product, service, or change? _____

_____

_____

4. Did you listen? _____

5. Did you make the adjustments or offered the product or service? Explain.

_____

_____

_____

Serving the Marketplace

How have you been making sure that you serving your clients the way that they need to be served?

_____

_____

_____

Canvassing the Marketplace

Have you been taking the time to canvas your competitors to see what they are offering and what their clients are requesting? What have they been saying?

_____

_____

_____

_____

_____

_____

_____

_____

Showing up with your US

Have you been putting forth an US mentality or are you make your brand and business all about you and your needs? Be honest and explain. _____

_____

_____

_____

_____

STRATEGIZE

1. Send out a survey to your clients and email list asking them what they want and how they want it delivered.
2. Ask questions on your social media platforms and record their responses.
3. When you post on a daily basis, pay attention to the comments.
4. When you attend networking events, have conversations that allow people to give you their insight and opinions about your industry.

EVALUATE

After you have implemented the strategies about, what have you learned about your industries needs that you were not aware of before implementing the strategies. What adjustments are you going to be making moving forward?

_____

_____

_____

_____

_____

_____

Law 14

The Law of Rejection

Rejection is the hardest thing for anyone of any age and industry to face. Being told "No," though not personal in most cases, should not be taken personally by those being told "No." "No, I don't want your product." "No, I don't want your service." The receiver hears these words as, "No, I don't like you." It takes a tough outer shell and sense of self to get past "No" as not being a rejection of you but instead a rejection of what you're offering.

In this section, we will explore how you deal with rejection, how you should deal with rejection, and the lessons you can learn from it.

REFLECT

1. How do you handle being rejected by others?

   _____

   _____

   _____

   _____

2. Do you currently have a recovery plan for when rejection really hits you hard?

   _____

3. Who do you turn to when you are rejected for advice? Why? _____

   _____

4. How do you turn that rejection into a positive? _____
_____
_____

STRATEGIZE

Come up with a strategy to handle rejection from other networkers, customers, and potential customers.

1. _____
_____
_____

2. _____
_____
_____

3. _____
_____
_____

4. _____
_____
_____

EVALUATE

What have you learned about yourself? _____
_____
_____
_____
_____
_____

Who are the people in your rejection support system now and how are they working out? _____

_____

_____

_____

_____

_____

_____

Do you find that preparing for rejection helps to make it easier to handle? Explain who and why or why not. _____

_____

_____

_____

_____

_____

_____

_____

_____

_____

_____

_____

_____

_____

_____

_____

_____

_____

Law 15
The Law of Preparation

Personal development is essential to the survival of any business owner and their business. We live in an age where things are constantly changing, and new innovations pop up weekly. The world is getting smaller because of the internet, and we must be prepared for anything at all times.

In this section, we will explore how personal development can influence your networking interactions.

REFLECT

1. How are you currently identifying the issues in your life that are or can potentially affect your ability to network effectively?

   _____

   _____

   _____

   _____

2. Do you currently read self-help books? Do you find that they help?

   _____

   _____

3. Have you seen a therapist or life coach to help you deal with the things that are bothering you? How has that been going? If not, would you consider seeing one?

   _____

   _____

   _____

   _____

Personal Development

Have you considered personal development in any of these areas? Explain what you have done in the past.

Self-help

_____

_____

Professional Development (Free or Paid) _____

_____

_____

Learning a New Language _____

_____

Learning a New Skill _____

_____

STRATEGIZE

If you are not currently partaking in any of the above, create a plan to do so. Write the plan below.

Seek out the services of a therapist _____

_____

_____

_____

_____

Analysis my interaction at networking events and how people respond to you and make adjustments independently or with professional assistance.

_____

_____

_____

_____

_____

Professional Development (Free or Paid) _____

_____

_____

_____

_____

Learning a New Language _____

_____

_____

_____

Learning a New Skill _____

_____

_____

_____

EVALUATE

How has all your strategies worked out for you? Detail you experience below.

_____

_____

_____

_____

_____

Law 16

The Law of the Language Barrier

As you expand your network, we will inevitably come across language barriers that will hinder your ability to conduct your business effectively if you are doing business to business (B2B) or business to clients (B2C). This language barrier is not just verbal; it is also physical and emotional.

In this section, we will explore verbal, physical, and emotional cues that may cause us to miss the mark when networking.

REFLECT

1. Are you good are recognizing the following cues? How do you deal with a person that is displaying negativity using each one?

   Verbal Cues

   _____

   _____

   _____

   Physical Cues

   _____

   _____

   _____

   Emotional Cues

   _____

   _____

   _____

2. What types of verbal, physical, or emotional cues do you know that you give off subconsciously? How do people react to it? (E.g. Are people always telling you to smile or asking you why you are mad because you have a serious resting face?)

_____

_____

_____

_____

_____

_____

STRATEGIZE

Device a strategy to deal with your verbal, physical, and emotional cues and people's responses to them.

Verbal Cues

_____

_____

_____

_____

Physical Cues

_____

_____

_____

_____

Emotional Cues

_____

_____

_____

_____

Device a strategy to deal with verbal, physical, and emotional cues that you encounter when networking and how you will deal with it.

Verbal Cues

_____

_____

_____

_____

Physical Cues

_____

_____

_____

_____

Emotional Cues

_____

_____

_____

_____

EVALUATE

Journal what you have discovered and what the revelations have evoked within you as it relates to tactic.

_____

_____

_____

_____

Law 17

The Law of Commitment & Trustworthiness

Trustworthiness and a commitment to a cause, idea, or organization will get you a ton of brownie points in the networking realm. People want to know that they can trust the people they meet to do business with, refer clients to, and build solid relationships with for future endeavors.

In this section, we will explore how being trustworthy and committed can be positive for your business and personal reputation and spill over into your interactions when networking.

REFLECT

1. What do you think the adjectives are that people are using to describe you when they are talking to other people about you and your business?

_____

_____

_____

_____

2. How do you think your reputation is affecting your business?

_____

_____

_____

3. Do you know someone that has a bad reputation both personally and professionally? How is it affecting their business?

_____

_____

_____

_____

_____

_____

4. Would you do business with someone that has a bad reputation or send them referrals? Why or why not?

_____

_____

_____

_____

Can You Be Counted On?

Do you have a reputation as someone that can be counted on? If not, is there anything that you have tried to solve this issue? Explain.

_____

_____

_____

_____

Long-term Relationships

Are you developing long-term personal or professional relationships or are you known as a user? Someone that takes from people what they want and need and then never reach back out to those people again after the deal is done. Be transparent. Reflect on things that others have said to you in the past to write a true reflection.

_____
_____
_____
_____
_____
_____
_____
_____
_____
_____

Gift Services - Use it

Do you follow up with people that have done you a favor, sent you a referral that paid off, or made a major impression on you by sending them a gift? If yes, what have you sent and why? If not, why haven't you done it? _____

_____
_____
_____
_____
_____
_____

STRATEGIZE

Create a strategy for doing better at the things above that you may be failing at currently.

_____
_____
_____

_____
_____
_____
_____
_____
_____
_____
_____

EVALUATE

What have you realized after implementation? What do you still need to tweak?

_____
_____
_____
_____
_____
_____
_____
_____
_____
_____
_____
_____
_____
_____
_____
_____

Law 18

The Law of Navigating the Space

We all know that networking is essential for the success of any business owner. No matter your profession, your industry, or demographic, the message is still the same – you need to network to get ahead. If you want to be successful, you need to spend time networking.

In this section, we will explore how to navigate through the networking space.

REFLECT

1. Where are you currently doing most of your networking? You can choose from the list provided in the chapter or add your own. How is that venue and group working for you? _____

_____

_____

_____

2. Have you tried any others? You should try as many as possible to make sure that you are not missing out on any opportunities. Give details here.

_____

_____

_____

_____

_____

Where Should I Network

What events, venues, or groups would you like to try and why? What have you heard about their process? _____

_____

_____

_____

Where can I add Value

How are you currently determining the value that you are receiving from you current networking circle? _____

_____

_____

NETWORKING VALUE ASSESSMENT

Networking Event	Person	Referral	Monetization	Assessment

View the Map from Above

Have you taken your feeling out of your current connections at the networking groups that you are affiliated with to assess the true value of the group? Use the chart above to help you with the assessment. What have you discovered?

_____

_____

_____

_____

_____

STRATEGIZE

Commit to analyzing each of your networking experiences to see if they are or were worth your time. Doing this will help you to make the most of your valuable time and you will only attend events that are beneficial. _____

_____

_____

_____

_____

_____

_____

_____

_____

_____

_____

_____

_____

EVALUATE

After doing the above steps, evaluate your results by comparing and contrasting them below? _____

_____

_____

_____

_____

_____

_____

_____

_____

_____

_____

_____

_____

_____

_____

_____

_____

_____

_____

_____

_____

_____

_____

_____

_____

_____

Law 19

The Law of Wisdom

Trust your gut! How many times have you heard this? How many times have you ignored that gut-wrenching feeling that kept nudging at you, telling you that there is something not trustworthy about someone you met at a networking event? How many times did you still follow up with that person, set up a coffee date, and try to prove your instincts wrong just to be disappointed because your gut instincts were right?

In this section, we will explore how wisdom can help you get ahead.

REFLECT

1. Have you ever met someone or went somewhere, and your gut just felt like it was being squeezed? That's the gut telling you that something isn't right. It has been said that the gut is the second brain, so you should listen to it. Have you had experiences where this has happened? Explain.

   _____
   _____
   _____
   _____
   _____
   _____
   _____
   _____

2. Have you second guessed your gut and it turned out to be a complete disaster? Explain. _____
   _____

_____

_____

_____

3. What have you learned from past experiences about yourself and following your gut?

_____

_____

_____

_____

_____

_____

4. Explain the outcome and what you learned from it.

_____

_____

_____

_____

_____

_____

STRATEGIZE

How do you intend to move forward with listening to your gut? Beyond just listening to the second brain, I use a system that listens, analyzes, and synthesizes what both the head brain and gut brain are saying. When in proper use the outcome will NOT be failure.

_____

_____

_____

_____

_____

_____

_____

_____

_____

_____

_____

_____

_____

_____

_____

_____

GUT ASSESSMENT

Gut Feeling	Research	Conclusion

EVALUATE

How has the combination of gut feelings backed by real facts equal to a sounder decision-making process? Share your thoughts. _____

_____

_____

_____

_____

_____

_____

_____

_____

_____

_____

_____

_____

_____

_____

_____

_____

_____

_____

_____

_____

_____

_____

_____

_____

_____

Law 20

The Law of Magnetism

The law of attraction in networking is simple, gravitate to the people who make sense for your business goals and objectives and the people that do good/ethical business for themselves.

In this section, we will explore how magnetism works in networking.

REFLECT

1. Has there been a person or event that you have been drawn to solely based on visuals or buzz? This is called magnetism. Describe the person or event and what drew you to it.

_____

_____

_____

_____

_____

_____

_____

2. Have you been able to connect with another human being on an extremely intimate level that garnered a lifetime relationship that was either business or personal?

_____

_____

_____

3. What was the draw to this person?

_____

_____

_____

4. Do you think it is possible to have that type of magnetism multiple times in your life? Why or why not? _____

_____

_____

5. Did all of your magnetic connections last or did you figure out that the person was just a mirage. Not what they appeared to be online or when you initially met them in person. Explain.

_____

_____

_____

_____

_____

_____

_____

STRATEGIZE

What is your strategy for assessing magnetism?

_____

_____

_____

_____

_____

Here's what I've used in the past. This can be used for both sexes. Remember, this is not about sex but a meaningful connection.

Person	Characteristics	What I find Attractive

EVALUATE

Have you been able to identify what characteristics created that spark/magmatism in the first true connection you made in that area? Explain.

_____

_____

_____

_____

_____

_____

_____

_____

_____

_____

_____

_____

_____

Law 21

The Law of the Circle

They say that we are all separated from someone that we want or need to meet by at least six people that we know. If we believe that to be true, why are we not in the rooms and around the people that we desire. That's simple! We are afraid to ask for what we want. We are so scared to ask for introductions to those people. We are afraid that the people we need to ask for those introductions are going to think that we are an opportunist, or we harbor self-doubt and worry. You may even ask yourself - "Who do I think I am? Why do I think I am good enough to sit amongst these people?"

In this section, we will explore what your circle can do to help you reach your desired goals and objectives for your business, career, and life.

REFLECT

1. Do you freak out when you have to ask someone to do you a favor? Does that anxiety come from not wanting to owe anyone anything?

   _____

   _____

2. Do you think this is a sustainable practice for a business owner?

   _____

   _____

3. When you do something for someone do you expect an immediate return on investment?

   _____

   _____

   _____

4. Have you asked your network to introduce you to someone else that you wanted to meet for business reasons? What was the reaction to the request? Did you get the introduction? How did it transpire and how did it conclude?

_____

_____

_____

_____

_____

_____

5. Do you readily give introductions when asked by your circle? Why or why not?

_____

_____

_____

_____

_____

_____

STRATEGIZE

Here are the strategies that you should use to maximize your networking circle. Write your own strategy for each one.

1. Know what you want out of your networking interactions. _____

_____

2. Know what you are bringing to the table. _____

_____

3. Research the networking groups that attract the type of people you need to mingle with to elevate your brand. _____

_____

_____

4. Never pitch at your first meeting. Flattery works well here. Build a solid relationship. _____

_____

_____

5. Follow up within 24-48 hours. _____

_____

_____

6. Do it yourself. Be bold and introduce yourself via email or phone. _____

_____

_____

_____

7. Brand and promote yourself in such a way that people you want to meet, want to meet you as well and will reach out to you. _____

_____

_____

_____

_____

_____

_____

_____

_____

_____

_____

_____

_____

EVALUATE

How have the strategies above worked for you?

_____
_____
_____
_____
_____
_____
_____
_____
_____
_____
_____
_____
_____
_____
_____
_____
_____
_____
_____
_____
_____
_____
_____
_____
_____
_____
_____
_____

Bonus

How has the 21 Irrefutable Laws of networking systems and processes that you have read about coupled with the activities that you have done in this workbook helped you to become a more effective networker.

_____

_____

_____

_____

_____

_____

_____

_____

_____

_____

_____

_____

_____

_____

_____

_____

_____

_____

_____

_____

_____

_____

What do you still need to work on? What are your strategies for getting it done?

_____
_____
_____
_____
_____
_____
_____
_____
_____
_____
_____
_____
_____
_____
_____
_____
_____
_____
_____
_____
_____
_____
_____
_____
_____
_____
_____
_____